Bloom.

Danielle Gibbins

BookLeaf
Publishing

India | USA | UK

Bloom. © 2022

Danielle Gibbins

All rights reserved.

Presentation by *BookLeaf Publishing*

Web: www.bookleafpub.com

E-mail: info@bookleafpub.com

ISBN: 9789357444408

First edition 2022

DEDICATION

To everyone that I'm lucky to know in this lifetime. To everyone whose hearts have once hurt. And to you, the one who helped me 'bloom'.

PREFACE

she is a flower
but also
the sun
that lets
her bloom
- Christiane Stark

Sunflower.

Please, my love, don't you worry about me.

As now I have learned a powerful lesson.

To never depend on another person.

When I can depend on myself with certainty.

After all, a sunflower only needs one single seed
in order to bloom.

Wind.

I am still not certain how we got here, yet here we are.

We stood strong together on the foundation of 'us' for all of those days.

How did it only take one harsh wind to cause 'us' to collapse?

I thought we were stronger than that.

I thought we were as tough as steel, melded together with titanium, and cast in iron for safe keeping.

Yet, here we are, and I am still not sure how.

Days pass into weeks pass into months.

The wind that came and tore us down is silent now…yet you remain a hurricane that whirls unrestrained within my heart.

Here I am. Still so sure, still so soft; taped together shards of glass still clinging to the

debris of the life that we had so beautifully
begun to build.

Here I am. Alone. And I'm still not quite sure
how.

Truth.

There is a lot that is said about relationships. So many of us constantly try to figure out, what even is 'real love'?

Hundreds of people spread across our lives. With their own experiences, understandings, and beliefs, about how and what our individual love stories should look like. Unique heartaches and damage and healing, affect the principles and standards that others believe we should all strive for.

Thousands of movies, circling around the story of two lovers. Will they, won't they? Will that obstacle keep them apart? Won't that controversy bring them together? Two lives, completely entwined through scripted scenes and plot twists. Everyone hooked on the drama - full of addictive unease and excitement.

Millions of TV shows, equally the same. This person, with that person, who then moves on to that other person. An entanglement of lies, comedy and romance. It somehow always works out in the end. No tragedy can keep true love apart, it seems.

Billions of songs, routinely inspired by both happiness and heartbreak. A complicated labyrinth of emotions, feelings, adventures, fantasies. The highs, the lows, the in between, and the straight out messy.

We are overloaded with a constant influx of what true love 'should' feel like. What a strong, stable relationship 'should' be like. What our love stories 'should' appear like, to everybody and everyone observing, and listening, and watching from our outside worlds. We wonder how they compare to the shows and the movies and the songs that surround us permanently. An indirect infusion of expectations and idealisations blended together - it makes it impossible for our own love relationships to match up to any of it.

An unachievable, unattainable narrative, where you doubt and ask your own love: 'will this ever be enough?'

However, 'true love', a real solid relationship, isn't about the drama, and the fireworks, and the unrealistic spectacular scenes that are thrust upon us every single waking day. It is much more simple than that - it is found in the calm.

In the happy-to-just-sit-and-be-with-you moments. In the my-life-is-so-much-better-just-by-knowing-you moments. In the I-appreciate-you-breathing-the-same-air-as-me moments. In all of those moments that you reach out to that person, and they show up. In all of those moments that you look, and see that person standing by your side. Them holding your hand as you walk up the street. Them finishing your sentence when you are stumbling on words. Them purely being present in your world, no matter how far or near. A real, solid relationship full of love, does not require anything more than the uncomplicated understanding of this truth: to know that you are blissfully happy, being intertwined with them in the simplicity of what you have.

To know THAT is what it should feel like...it's the rest of the world that has got it wrong.

Home.

It all happened so quickly, didn't it? We met. We danced. We stumbled a little. Then we fell into the whirlwind of everything that was intriguing. We fell straight into one another.

We had fallen in love amongst the pebbles of that city we both adored so deeply; a plan that neither of us had made.

Before we had even caught out breaths, our lives became intertwined within the space of one another. It was exhilarating. Like nothing either of us had experienced in our lives before.

Wherever you were, that was exactly where I wanted to be. An abundance of adventures ahead. Laid before us, a road that glistened so enticingly. A road that was so natural for us both to take.

I remember once or twice, my head told me to slow this down. It's too soon. Too fast. I need some time alone. Yet my heart disregarded every alert; as I had somehow already built a home within you.

Throughout it all, you were the one, familiar place where I could reside. A home in lands that were completely new to me. You were my safe space. A place of warmth, of beauty, of everything that felt right.

Even now, when I lose myself in thoughts of 'you', in memories of 'us' - they still feel like home.

A home that I let myself stay in every once in a while. A place that I know I will visit less and less as the days, and the months, and the years go by. But still a place that I will always remember how it felt to live there.

Because really, how could I not? As when I close my eyes and think of 'home'...

I still see your face so clearly.

Change.

For me, there is only one, universal concept that I believe to be accurate for us all without exception - that change really is the only, one true constant in life.

Each year, each month, each day – plans change, people change, lives change.

We cannot with absolute certainty count on anything to stay the same, and why would we want it to?

With change, comes movement and shifts...what follows is growth.

With change, comes unease and surprises...what follows is expansion.

With change, comes fear and turbulence...what follows is joy.

We can bury our heads in the sand, hold on tight to our lives with every ounce of our strength. We can fight to refuse to let change affect us. Keep the same circle of people in our lives. Visit the same places. Keep up with the routine. We can try and try and try...yet change will always be inevitable.

There is simply no way to avoid it. So you may as well open up and welcome it in.

Because after change, beautiful beginnings follow.

There are new stories to share, new lessons to learn.

It might be that you need to change a lot more than you realize.

It might well be that change will provide the shining light to see what you were dreaming of all along.

Most.

I want you to know that I am (mostly) okay.

Everything changed a small while ago when you decided 'we' weren't what you wanted anymore. I was left voiceless, no choice in the matter. You changed my whole world, when you decided this for us both. All I could do was pick myself up, push on, and begin to adapt to this new life without 'you'.

I have had my share of the spiraling moments, there is no denying that. It has been a process. Gritty at times, perplexing at times. A real mosaic of a process. Still, I am (mostly) okay.

Then sometimes, just sometimes, I'll let myself get lost in the thoughts of 'you', in the memories of 'us', all over again.

I'll hear songs that carry me straight back to being held by you. My body intertwined in yours, hands clasped tightly together, our faces touching; me, wrapped comfortably in the nook of you.

I'll reminisce about the countless adventures.
The trips, the people, the spaces we shared. The
memories where we would laugh and learn and
leap from place to place. We would hold hands
every single day – down streets, through car
rides, everywhere, if even for just a moment.

I'll remind myself of words we gave to one
another. Words that will be forever etched into
my mind. 'I love you, most'. These thoughts
circle my mind, and bring a sense of nostalgia of
a love that surely could never expire. Promises
of future potential plans. Dreams that have since
turned to nothing more than clouds in the sky.

I try not to let myself get lost in this space often.
Yet when I do, it's almost impossible to not
reopen that heart-wound a little. A revived
insight to that cherished, abundant love that we
so recently shared. That love that you somehow
let slip right through your hands as you let me
go.

Despite these engulfing moments, and the
outpouring of my heart feels, I promise you, that
I really am (mostly) okay. And I honestly will
always hope that you are too.

Save.

And after the rain started to slow, it all started to make sense.

This wasn't only to save you,

It was to save me, too.

Trust.

'Trust the process' - words that were engraved permanently on my mind from the moment I first heard them not so long ago.

Guidance. To have faith that the unforeseen circumstances I found myself catapulted into were leading to something greater. Something bigger. Something more magical than I could ever have desired.

Advice. To trust that recent events are a part of an extraordinary transformation; a spellbinding rebirth of myself, and of life as I knew it.

Encouragement. To witness with loving acceptance, the mystical unfolding of the next part of my alluring story.

To trust with every part of my being, that everything is always, always working out for me. That there are no coincidences. That life will evolve, exactly how it is meant to. That the universe is looking out for me, and it has my best interests at heart. To know, deep down, that

I will continually be okay. That this is exactly where I am meant to be.

'Trust the process' they said, and trust it, I will.

Story.

I have come to understand that there may always be those rare moments, where the sadness suffocates my heart all over again.

An unpredictable reminder of you, of us. Where the concealed heartache rises to the surface once more.

Yet despite those occasional painful days.

I will never regret a single minute I had with you.

As our story will always be a remarkable one to tell.

So, please know that I will embrace those hard tremors every once in a while.

For they will forever be a comforting reminder that it was all real in the first place.

Forgive.

Hard things happen, every single day. There surely is not a human alive that has not experienced some kind of hurt and pain. Emotional, or physical, or a consolidation of them both.

Likewise, there are likely not many of us that have not caused discomfort for somebody else. Intentional, or unavoidable, or regrettably, an unfortunate blend of the two.

A friend, too busy to hang out on the weekend. A parent, too tired to hear about your day. A lover, too fragile to share a part of them anymore.

It is easy to let our hurt emotions affect our mood. To feel pity for ourselves. To blame our feelings on the very person that has caused us anguish.

To be mad, to be angry. To resent that person that we care so deeply for. To be frustrated that they were able to disrupt our flow.

It is easy to let the hurt cloud our thoughts, and ruin our day, and cause tears to stream down our cheeks.

Yet we can come to realize this. That no matter how hurt we feel, it is us, that are ultimately the ones that have the option to change our course. We can choose to be sad; we can choose to let our experiences harm us.

Or, we can stand tall and strong, and refuse to let them break us.

We can appreciate those difficulties for the growing moments that they provide.

We can respond with kindness, with understanding.

We can take the opportunity, and accept it for its learning value.

We can look past the suffering and the pain and the hurt.

We can turn to that person, who we care so deeply for, and we can respond with the most powerful action of all...
We can forgive them.

Dream.

And if it is only in my dreams that I get to see you,

Then I promise, I will always try to meet you there,

Every once in a while.

Soul.

I want you to know that I do not resent you for leaving 'us'. Neither do I hate you for breaking 'us'. I never could.

I heard you when you told me that this was what you needed for your own self. You needed to learn how to stand alone. How to fight your own shadows. How to breathe just for you.

Occasionally, I'll let myself get swallowed up once more in the raw emotion of it all. I fall into a mournful slumber, rocked by the aftershocks of disbelief that 'we' are no more all over again.

Yet, when the spiral levels out, my thoughts turn to silence, and my body returns to calmness. It is then that it remembers the truth. That despite those rare, messy, complicated, soul-churning moments of chaos that strike me in my very depths – your happiness still means so much to me. And all I truly want is for you to be happy.

So go, spread yourself wide, and set sail on that ocean of self-discovery. Reach inside to the

murky, hidden, corners of your being, and do
what you need, just for 'you'.

Because, my dear, I understand that is what you
need for your own soul.

And I can never resent you for caring about
yourself, the way that I will always care about
you too.

Rain.

We can grasp on to people, ideas, places, so tight that our hands turn red.

We can fight until dawn to prevent our plans, our direction, our lives, being influenced by change.

We can exhaust ourselves, leave ourselves motionless, trying to keep things 'just as they are'.

In what we know. Where we are comfortable. Where we are at peace.

Although, if we play it safe, if nobody leaves us, if we never alter our minds, if we rarely move places, if plans don't transform, if directions aren't swayed, if nothing ever changes...we could deny ourselves of so much potential, just for more of the same.

Without being faced with chaos, without challenge, without the threat of figuring-it-all-out to survive, we are blind to the scope of our inner strength. Our resilience would tremble. Without the risk of the unpredictable

unknown, we would never understand how
mesmerizing things could turn out.

There would be no surprises, no heart-flutters of
bewilderment for what could possibly unfold
next. There would be no unfolding of dreams
bigger than what we could have envisioned.

If things stay 'just as they are', we would never
know what magic we are truly capable of.

After all, flowers only bloom when there's a
little rain.

So,
let,
the rain,
POUR.

You.

To every person who has had lost someone that they adore,

Please remember this.

That to love somebody else,

You have to feel that love within yourself in the first place.

Universe.

Questions of what happened to us have traveled my mind on repeat. As routine as the planets that orbit the sun.

The hows. The whys. The would haves, could haves, should haves.

Trying to make sense of the collapse of our life together on Earth as we knew it. Of the collapse of 'us'.

We tumbled through the cosmos into the isolated black hole that lay secretly lurking in the darkness, unbeknown to the both of us.

We lost sight of our dreams, our goals, our stars, our light.

Then, it happened. Just how it started with the universe that holds us all together...a big bang.

A change of everything.

A shift occurred. A shift in me.

I found myself abruptly fired into somewhere
entirely new.

An awakening. Shooting stars. A milky way
swirling the skies of opportunity around me.

Everything looks different now.

There is no 'us' here...there is only 'me'.

Now I am not just the moon that orbits the
planet of 'you'. I am the sun. I shine on my own.
I am the brightest star in the night sky.

I am beaming, and for that I thank you.

The lesson is as clear as stardust to me now.
That we must always appreciate the complex
flurry of galaxies that we hold within our own
selves.

We do not need to rely on anyone, as nothing is
outside of us. Everything we could ever need
can be found within ourselves.

We are our whole entire damn universe already.

Love.

'Love' - one of the most expressed feelings in all languages. Communicated through different words and sounds by billions of us, every single day.

'I love you'.
'I love this'.
'I love us'.

If you have been told that you are loved by somebody you adore, you do not forget those moments easily. If at all ever.

You remember everything about those words. They are not just spoken to you; you feel them echo through your whole body.

The way they fall around you and on you and in you. The way they hold your hand, and soothe your wounds, and warm your soul. The way they spark smiles with your eyes. The way they make your heart vibrate with emotion yet feel calm with security, all in the same second. The way they elevate you and heal you and shake you and soften you.

Those words, they grip you in all of the ways possible when they are said by somebody you truly, truly cherish. A form of willing captivation at its best.

Then, one day, that person you honor so fiercely, they leave. The words stop altogether. For a deep, dark moment they will feel nothing more than a lost, disorientated, and distant memory.

Yet, the beautiful truth is this; that silence? That silence changes nothing.

Once you are connected through love; you are connected through it all.

Your hearts.
Your bodies.
Your mind.

You are collectively combined through the pieces of you both. Forever intertwined in the synchronicities of the universe that you will share infinitely.

Love knows no distance, no boundaries. Love's energy cannot be transferred or shattered or destroyed.

Love is them, and love is you. Whether together, or apart.

To truly love, is to love without conditions, or motive, or gain. To have received it back for even just a moment, is enough to solidify that connection indefinitely.

Close your eyes, tune in intently, and you will always feel it.

Let it resonate throughout your whole aching body.

Because, this love, it is forever yours to keep.

Sea.

Imagine.

That you are a part of the remarkable, sapphire seas that cover our world.

Most days, you can lie silently still. Drifting on the restful, heavenly water.

Harmonious, tranquil. You feel calm in the gentle, soothing waves. Watching with content as the clouds drift high above you. Floating without disturbance.

Peaceful. It all feels so peaceful.

Then, every once in a while, without any warning, those very same waves smash down on you with tremendous force. Flooding your space, momentarily holding you underwater, as though you are incapable of swimming up for air.

Those days, they are the hard ones. They feel impossible. They leave you petrified that you

would not survive the fierce force of another one
of them.

Yet, they are the ones where you learn to swim
again. They are the ones that make the steady
days feel so extraordinary.

So, when those hard waves crash down on you -
kick like your life depends on it. Because, in one
way, it does.

That sweet peaceful sea, it will always, always
return.

No matter how much it feels as though you are
drowning in the ocean depths. Keep on kicking -
I promise you it will be worth it.

Showtime.

Life truly is a book. A play. A story you get to write with your own ideas and decisions and choices. A range of narratives at your mind's fingertips. You wait patiently to watch the next episode you wrote play out.

Usually, you are both the author of the story, and the director of the show. Although, sometimes, on those rare and inopportune occasions, you find yourself suddenly propelled into an undesired front row seat of a crowded audience.

You watch with apprehension, as a dramatic story plays out on stage by actors with your face and her face and the faces of those that you love. You are still in the center of it all, yet you are not directing the scene anymore.

You didn't write this chapter, you didn't draft this one up. As hard as you try to control the action before you, you cannot edit this one out.

Twists of words and turns of directions and unwanted choices and before you know it...the

orchestras playing. End scene. The curtains
close. The story ends. What?

To you it was still only the beginning of the play.
You didn't sign up for a cliffhanger.

Nobody else wanted this.

Least of all you.

Ego.

'You deserve better'.
Although, what if I don't crave this idea of a
'better' something that they foresee?
What if the real truth is, that the world only says
this as a way to try to protect me.
My ego, their egos, reflected back through their
considerate words of protection.

'You don't need to put up with that'.
A sympathetic attempt to ensure my fragile heart
will avoid more hurt.
What if it is already hurting? Better yet, what if
it is already healing?

'Know your worth'
But here's the thing, I promise you, I honestly
already know it.

What if, instead of succumbing to fear and
worry, we tear down those guarded walls, throw
the ego aside, and set down our heart armor.

If we strip ourselves of the wrath of the ego, all
that is left bare is the complete adoration for
your person; an undeniable pure, profound love.

A love that stands still so raw and strong, it does
not desire any protection.
That kind of love, it is undefeatable.

The ego, if we choose to let it, has no lasting
hold on the true, irrefutable breath of the heart.
If we allow it, the heart will stand confident in
all its beauty. Beating proud, and so very, very
sure.

For some of us, it is the most truthful muscle of
all.

Magic.

If only you could see yourself, the way that I see you;

A magnetic force, with charisma in your veins.

If you could understand how your presence charges the room,

You would never doubt yourself again;

As nobody creates magic, quite like you do.

Strength.

Every single person experiences darkness from time to time. Heartbreak, grief, loneliness. A collapse of your universe that happens right before your eyes, catapulting you into the murkiness of it all.

In those times, in those low moments where it is hard, where it is a struggle…please always know that strength can be gained from an abundance of measures. However insignificant something may seem.

It can be pulled from your regular café barista, knowing your order when they see you approach. Smiling that smile, insinuating that serving you is part of their expected and welcomed daily routine.

It can come from curling up on the sofa with a treasured childhood movie. Observing those familiar faces and stories that you remember so well. Reciting the words that you have heard countless times before.

It can be reached through playing an angsty music album from your teenage years full blast in the safety of your car, and shouting along without fail to every single word.

It can be felt through a work colleague confiding in you that they too, have had their hard moments. That brief, but true, empathetic connection, can provide a stepping stone of strength from the haunting feeling that you have at the base of your stomach. Bridging bonds that will stand tall when brighter days return.

It can be absorbed through the scribbling of your thoughts and feelings on paper. Splashing the words with tears as you let it all out. Nobody needs to decipher it, once it's out there, that's all that is needed. A physical release of mental discomfort. Processed, then expended. Strength gained through the surrender of buried beliefs, fears, and pain that you kept shielded behind your eyes.

It can be drawn through providing yourself with some kind of self-care: ordering take-out from that same favorite, familiar place you've visited since you were a child; letting yourself cry hysterically, holding your own arms around your body without judgment; or by admitting that you are not your brightest self right now, and accepting that is more than okay.

Strength, in one of the greatest and most immense ways, can also be found in the people you are fortunate to share your world with. Old friends, new friends, family. All those people who rally behind you, when they recognise you need it most.

Messages to let you know that you are thought about, cared about. Calls when you wake up, on their lunch breaks, during their evenings, so that you can hear a recognizable voice. The unexpected surprises through flowers, books, plants, and cards of support. Being taken out for walks along the beach, on bushwalks, or even concrete streets, to provide you with a safe space to share the pain with them, to gain even just a fraction of release. They provide compassion, and validate your thoughts. They prevent you from feeling alone. They connect with you in those hard-to-deal moments when it counts, embrace you with their love, and send warm hugs straight from their body to yours, whether they're physically present or not.

These gold-hearted, pure types of people, omit strength directly straight from themselves to

you, by simply being present. They are solid
pillars of substantial strength, every single one
of them.

To all of these extraordinary angel-on-earth type
people who have provided me with even a
moment of strength; please know that I thank
you with every piece of my heart, and I will be
forever grateful to know you, always xx